Collins
INTERNATIONAL

T0337722

Science
Foundation Plus
Anthology

Published by Collins
An imprint of HarperCollins*Publishers*
The News Building, 1 London Bridge Street,
London, SE1 9GF, UK

HarperCollins*Publishers*
Macken House, 39/40 Mayor Street Upper,
Dublin 1, DO1 C9W8, Ireland

Browse the complete Collins catalogue at
www.collins.co.uk

10 9 8 7 6 5 4 3

ISBN 978-0-00-846892-7

British Library Cataloguing-in-Publication Data
A catalogue record for this publication is available from the British Library.

Compiled by: Fiona Macgregor
Publisher: Elaine Higgleton
Product manager: Letitia Luff
Commissioning editor: Rachel Houghton
Researcher: Andi Colombo
Edited by: Eleanor Barber
Editorial management: Oriel Square
Cover designer: Kevin Robbins
Cover illustrations: Jouve India Pvt Ltd.
Internal illustrations: Jouve India Pvt. Ltd., p 5 Stu Mclellan,
p 26–27 Nathalie Ortega, p 29–31 Tasneem Amiruddin
Typesetter: Jouve India Pvt. Ltd.
Production controller: Lyndsey Rogers
Printed and Bound in the UK using 100% Renewable
Electricity at Martins the Printers

Acknowledgements

With thanks to all the kindergarten staff and their schools around the world who
have helped with the development of this course, by sharing insights and
commenting on and testing sample materials:

Calcutta International School: Sharmila Majumdar, Mrs Pratima Nayar, Preeti
Roychoudhury, Tinku Yadav, Lakshmi Khanna, Mousumi Guha, Radhika Dhanuka,
Archana Tiwari, Urmita Das; Gateway College (Sri Lanka): Kousala Benedict; Hawar
International School: Kareen Barakat, Shahla Mohammed, Jennah Hussain; Manthan
International School: Shalini Reddy; Monterey Pre-Primary: Adina Oram; Prometheus
School: Aneesha Sahni, Deepa Nanda; Pragyanam School: Monika Sachdev; Rosary
Sisters High School: Samar Sabat, Sireen Freij, Hiba Mousa; Solitaire Global School:
Devi Nimmagadda; United Charter Schools (UCS): Tabassum Murtaza; Vietnam
Australia International School: Holly Simpson

The publishers wish to thank the following for permission to reproduce photographs.

(t = top, c = centre, b = bottom, r = right, l = left)

p 2–3 Will Amlot, p 9b Neil McAllister/Alamy Stock Photo, p 18tl Discovery Channel
Images/Getty Images, p 18tr Japan Images/Tohoku Color Agency/Getty Images,
p 18cl mauritius images GmbH/Alamy Stock Photo, p 18cr Jason Edwards//National
Geographic Society/Getty Images, p 18bl Andre Baertschi/Photoshot/NHPA, p 18br
Simon Williams/naturepl.com, p 19tl WILDLIFE GmbH/Alamy Stock Photo, p 19tr
Philippe Clement/naturepl.com, p 19cl David Boag/Alamy Stock Photo, p 19cr Peter
Arnold/Getty Images, p 19bl Alaska Stock/Alamy Stock Photo, p 19br Juniors
Tierbildarchiv/Photoshot, p 24–25 Tim Platt. All other photographs: Shutterstock.

MIX
Paper | Supporting
responsible forestry
FSC™ C007454

This book is produced from independently
certified FSC™ paper to ensure responsible
forest management.

For more information visit:
www.harpercollins.co.uk/green

I am a scientist

We look closely.

We use equipment safely.

We measure.

We talk about what we see.

Myself and others

Have you eaten any of these?
Which ones do you like?

What are the children doing?

My senses

I see.

I touch.

I taste.

I hear.

I smell.

Animals

Which animals are these?

Plants

Seeds grow into plants.

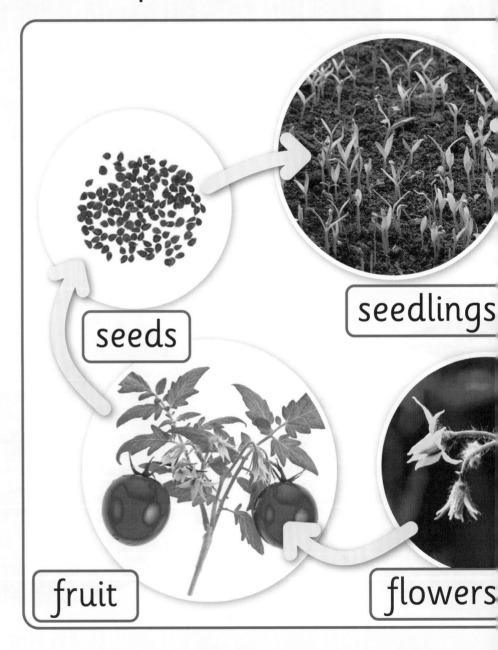

seeds

seedlings

fruit

flowers

plants

What plants and animals need

Animals need food, water, air and shelter.

Plants need soil, water,
air and sunlight.

water

sunlight

soil

Habitats

Some plants grow underwater.

Some plants grow on land.

Solids and liquids

Water can be a solid.

Water can be a liquid.

Does it sink or float?

Growing and changing

What is in the eggs?

Animals grow and change.

Light and dark

The sun shines in the day.
It gives us light and heat.

At night, we see the moon.

We see the moon change shape.

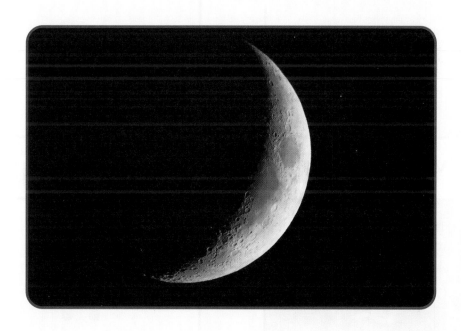

Weather

What is the weather like today?

Sunday

sunny

Monday

cloudy

Tuesday

rainy

Wednesday

windy

Thursday

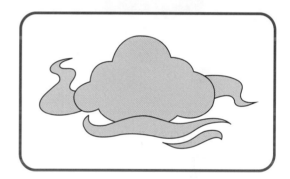

foggy

Friday and
Saturday

snowy

Materials

How to make a maraca.

1

Put the pasta in a pot.

2

Put glue around the top of the pot.

3

Stick another pot on top.

4

Cut up a piece of paper.

Put glue on the piece
of paper.

Wrap the paper around
your pots. Use tape.

Decorate your maraca.

Play with your maraca.

Taking care of our world

It is a big mess.

Pick up the mess.

Fill up a bag.

Put the bags in the bins.

Pushes and pulls

I push.

I pull.

Changing materials

We have a pot, pot, pot.
It is hot, hot, hot.

We have ice, ice, ice.
It is nice, nice, nice.

We have a tray, tray, tray.
We like to play, play, play.

What will it be, be, be?
We wait and see, see, see.

I know about:

☐ being a scientist

☐ myself and others

☐ using my senses

☐ animals

☐ plants

☐ what plants and animals need

☐ habitats of animals

☐ solids and liquids

☐ growing and changing

☐ light and dark

☐ the weather

☐ materials

☐ taking care of our world

☐ pushes and pulls

☐ changing materials.